EASY MAGIC TRICKS

25 BEGINNER MAGIC TRICKS WITH EVERYDAY OBJECTS

SAM FURY

Illustrated by
NEIL GERMIO

WARNINGS AND DISCLAIMERS

CONTENTS

ELASTIC BANDS

THANKS FOR YOUR PURCHASE

Did you know you can get FREE chapters of any SF Nonfiction Book you want?

https://offers.SFNonfictionBooks.com/Free-Chapters

You will also be among the first to know of FREE review copies, discount offers, bonus content, and more.

Go to:

https://offers.SFNonfictionBooks.com/Free-Chapters

Thanks again for your support.

INTRODUCTION

This book has 25 impromptu magic tricks you can perform with various small objects. All of the tricks require minimal or no setup, and none require gimmicks (special props) to work.

The book is split into five sections, each focusing on a different type or small object. They are:

- Coins
- Rings
- Pens
- Straws
- Elastic bands

Since all the tricks in this book are setup- and gimmick-free, you can do them with objects you find lying around, as opposed to having to purchase or make a special item to make them work.

Some of the effects will only work with the object they are demonstrated with in the trick. With others, the object can be replaced with similar things. For example, you can use:

- Coins for small rocks
- Elastic bands for hair ties
- Pens for straws

TERMINOLOGY

Here is a list of magic-specific terminology used in this book.

- **Dominant hand**: The hand you are most comfortable using for common acts, such as writing.
- **Non-dominant hand**: The hand that isn't your dominant hand.
- **Trick**: A single effect in a sequence.
- **Finishing clean**: Finishing a trick with no evidence of how you did it.
- **Flashing**: Unintentionally showing an object or technique.
- **Gimmick**: A prop, of which the spectator is unaware, used to make a trick possible.
- **Method**: How you perform a trick.
- **Patter**: What you say while performing a trick.
- **Palming**: Holding an object in your palm so it is out of your spectator's view.
- **Reveal**: The part of a trick that shows something "magical" has happened.
- **Sequence**: A number of tricks performed one after another.
- **Setup**: An action you need to do before performing a trick in order to make the trick work.
- **Sleight**: A technique used to help make the trick work.
- **Spectator**: The person for whom you are performing the trick.

BASIC PRINCIPLES OF MAGIC

Here are some fundamental principles that will help you in all areas of magic.

Not all of these principles of magic will apply to every trick, but in general, adhering to them will make your sleights, tricks, and sequences better.

Misdirection

Misdirection is when you draw your spectator's attention to one thing to prevent him from noticing another.

There are two basic ways to do this. The first encourages the spectator to look away. Some examples of this are to:

- Look up so the spectator follows your eyes.
- Ask him to think of or memorize something.
- Use patter so he looks at you instead of your hands.

The second method of redirection is to use a larger movement to cover the smaller one. The idea of this to make the spectator think the larger movement contains the secret, so he will not pay attention to how the real sleight is happening.

Same Actions

Use the same action when doing a sleight as you would when doing the action normally. If you use one action to do something and then another when doing a sleight, it looks suspicious.

Patter

Patter is what you say throughout a trick and/or sequence of tricks. It has several uses:

- **Misdirection.** Engaging patter can distract your spectator from things you do want him to see.
- **Memory aid.** Creating a story will help you remember the sequence of slights in a trick and/or the order of tricks in your sequence.
- **Flow.** Jumping from one trick to another without a story to connect them can be awkward. Using patter will help things move along smoothly.
- **Gives a reason.** Sometimes you need to do a certain action to make a trick work, but doing so without a reason would look out of place. Use patter to fill that void.
- **Entertainment.** Having an engaging story to go with your tricks adds entertainment value. Adapting your patter to your personality will help with this as well.

A Light Touch

Learning the sleights needed for close-up magic can be challenging to begin with. You may need to build up dexterity to achieve certain movements.

A common mistake people make is being too rigid or gripping too hard. When you are having trouble with a certain technique, try using a lighter touch. As you get better, aim to make your finger movements as minimal as possible and fix things that look awkward or out of place.

Angles

For some sleights, such as vanishes, angles become increasingly important.

Consider carefully how you position your hands and body in relation to your spectator's line of sight. Using a mirror and/or recording yourself on video can help you pinpoint the best angles to use.

Tapping the Wand

Tapping the wand is a metaphor for having a reason for the "magic" to happen, such as tapping the object with a wand. Without this type of gesture, your reveal has less impact, and in some cases, the spectator may not even realize something magical happened.

The are many ways to "tap the wand," limited only to your imagination. Here are some examples that either you or your spectator can do:

- Tap the object with your pen or a finger.
- Snap your fingers.
- Wave your hand over the object.
- Shout a direction at the object, such as "rise."
- Hit down on the object with your hand.

Keeping it Magical

When a spectator sees a well-performed trick for the first time, he gets a sense of amazement. But as soon as he discovers how you did it, the amazement in that trick, and all the following ones, dissipates. This is why you should never reveal your secrets to your spectator.

Besides not actually revealing your methods, here are some tips on how to keep your tricks secret:

- **Don't show the same trick twice.** The first time you show someone a trick, he has no idea what is going to happen. The second time, he knows what to expect and will be looking for how it works.
- **Don't use the same technique too often.** The more times a spectator sees a specific sleight, the more likely he is to figure out how you did it. Instead, learn several ways to achieve the same result and interchange them throughout your sequence.
- **Practice a lot before performing**. Except for the most

basic ones, you need to practice any single trick at least 10 times before you can try performing it, or your spectator is likely to catch on to your method.

- **Downplay mistakes**. Mistakes happen. You may drop something or flash your technique. If you don't make a big deal about it, neither will your spectator. You can make a joke about it, or otherwise incorporate it into your patter so the spectator thinks it is part of the performance. Alternatively, just acknowledge it and move on.

COINS

FRENCH DROP VANISH

The French drop is a basic sleight of hand you can use to make any small object disappear.

Method

Cradle the coin with your thumb, index, and middle fingers so it is horizontal.

Come over with your other hand as if you are grabbing the coin. As you make the grabbing motion, use your thumb of your grabbing hand to push up on the thumb of your coin hand, so that the coin drops into your palm.

As you pull away your empty hand (which your spectator thinks the coin is in), turn over the hand with the coin and palm it.

At the same time, open your hand to reveal the coin has vanished. This is a reveal and misdirection.

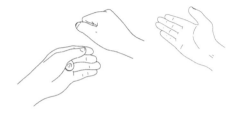

Do whatever you want with the coin. For example:

- Put it in your pocket.
- Drop it on the ground and step on it.
- Drop it in your lap.
- Make it reappear from your spectator's shirt pocket (or somewhere else).

NAPKIN VANISH

This is an easy vanish to do at a bar or dinner table when you have a napkin handy. You rub the coin into the table and then it vanishes.

Method

Wipe your hands or the table with a paper napkin, and then place it on the table next to where you want to do the trick. This allows you to position the napkin without suspicion, as well as to crumple it up a bit, which makes the trick work better.

Do it far from the edge of the table to make it more believable.

With the coin flat on the table, place your index finger and thumb on top of it and start moving it in a circle.

After a few rotations and when it is close to the napkin, use your thumb to "kick it" under the napkin.

You can start with big circles and gradually get smaller until you finally reveal the coin is gone.

COIN SWAP

In this trick, you hold a coin in each hand and then slam your hands on a flat surface. When you lift your hands, one of the coins has been transported to the other hand.

Method

You need two coins, one in each hand. It is best to do this on a soft surface to prevent damage.

Hold one coin in the palm of your hand, and the other just beneath the tip of your middle finger on your other hand. Turn your hands over and slam them on the surface simultaneously.

Do it so the coin in your fingertips is thrown underneath your other hand.

Reveal that the coin in one hand has now disappeared. Then reveal that it has been transported to the other hand.

COIN TO PEN LID

With this trick, you use a pen as a wand to make a coin in your hand disappear instantly. You then shake the pen cap and the coin falls out of it.

Method

You need a pen and a coin for this trick.

Place the coin in your palm and hold the pen like a wand in your other hand. Tap the pen lid on the coin a couple of times. On the last tap, toss the coin from your open hand into the hand holding the pen.

Take off the pen lid with the hand that has the coin in it and shake it, with the open end towards your empty palm. On the last shake, let the coin drop into your empty hand.

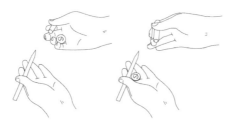

COIN THROUGH TABLE

In this trick, you pick up a coin and tap it on the table. After the few taps, the coin disappears and passes though the table into your other hand.

Method

For this trick you need to be seated at an opaque table with a coin on it. Pick the coin up by sliding it to the edge of the table and grasping it between your two fingers and thumb.

Show the spectator the coin and, as you drop it back on the table, say you are going to make it go through the table.

Pick up the coin again in the same manner, but this time, flick the coin down into your lap and just pretend to pick it up. Grab the coin with your other hand and use it to tap the bottom of the table as you pretend to tap the coin on the top of the table. Make sure the taps have the same timing as the action for the auditory bluff.

After a few taps, act as if you are pushing the coin into the table. When you want it to "go through," do a single harder tap.

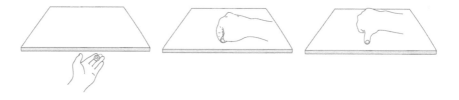

Show the coin is missing from the top of the table, then bring your other hand out to reveal it.

TRANSPORTING COINS

In this trick, four coins are displayed on a table. You place your hand over them, and one by one, they move from one hand to the other.

Method

You need five of the same coins and a soft surface. The surface needs to be soft so the coins don't make noise when they are moving. Placing a towel on a table will work.

Place four of the coins in a square on the table. Hide the fifth coin on the table under one of your hands. Ensure all five coins are facing the same way (either face up or face down).

Display your empty hands by moving the hand hiding the coin forward a bit so that the coin is under your wrist. Turn both hands over to show them empty. Use the palm of your hand to drag the hidden coin to the coin in the top right-hand corner of the table.

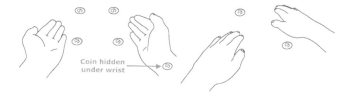

Leave the coin there, and at the same time, use your other hand to drag the bottom left-hand coin backwards.

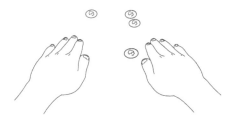

Slide the coin in your left hand to the top right and leave it there with the other two. At the same time, drag the bottom right-hand coin away with your right hand.

Do the same thing with the last coin.

Turn both hands over to show them empty, with the fifth coin under your wrist. Alternatively, slide the fifth coin down into your lap.

COIN SNAP CHANGE

In this trick, you hold a coin in your fingers, and with a wave of your hand, it instantly transforms into a different coin.

Method

Get two coins of different sizes. Hold them between your thumb and index finger, so that the larger coin is facing your spectator, with the smaller coin behind it.

Bring you other hand over and wave it in front of the coins. With your spectator's view blocked by your hand, extend your middle finger in front of the coins.

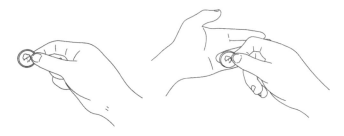

Pull the larger coin back into your palm. Finish with your fingers in the same position you started in.

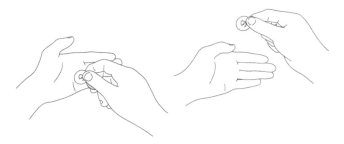

RINGS

RING APPEARS IN HAND

In this move, you display your empty hand and then magically pull a ring out of it.

Method

Hold your hand facing your spectator, with your wrist tilted up a little. Place the ring behind your thumb. Make it as close as you can, so it can balance without being in view.

Bring your other hand over as if you are grasping something from inside the ring hand, then wrap your ring hand around the fingers of your grasping hand.

With your four fingers covering your spectator's view, use your thumb to slide the ring inside your hand.

Slowly open your hand to show the ring has appeared.

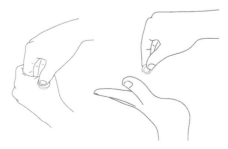

RING JUMPS TO FINGER

In this trick, you take a ring off your finger then throw it back on through your finger from underneath.

Method

Start with the ring on your index finger. Hold your hand in a fist, with your index finger stretched out. Show the ring to your spectator so that the palm of your ring hand is facing you.

Bring your other hand over as if to take the ring off. As it comes over, rotate your ring hand to a palm-down position. Your non-ring hand hides your first and the middle fingers of your ring hand from the spectator's view.

As you as you rotate your ring hand, bring your index finger in and extend your middle finger.

Act as if you are pulling the ring off your middle finger. Your spectator will think the ring is in your hand, but it is still on your index finger.

Bring your non-ring hand below your ring hand and act as if you are throwing the ring up.

As you make the throwing action, move your ring hand up and down as you switch back to your index finger. The up-down action will blur the switch.

RING THROUGH FINGER

In this trick, you take a ring off by pulling it through your finger.

Method

The ring you use for this trick must fit on your ring finger without being too tight.

Position your ring hand so both your palm and the tip of your ring finger are is pointing up. Bring your other hand over your finger to grab the ring between your thumb and fingers. Tug on the ring a couple of times to show it can't get through your finger. On the final tug, relax your finger and tilt the ring up.

Bend your ring finger down as you lift the ring off. You don't want to move either your finger or your hand too much. Move them about the same amount, which should be as little as possible. Return your finger to its original position as fast as possible so the ring ends up in the original position in relation to it.

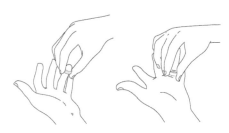

RING THROUGH CORD

In this trick, a piece of cord is threaded through a ring. You pull the ring off through the cord, then make it reappear.

Method

For this trick, you need a ring and some type of cord, such as a shoelace, string, or headphones.

Thread the ring to about the center of the cord, then hold it in between your thumb and index finger of your right hand. The back of your hand should face your spectator.

Bring your left hand over to grab the ring. Your thumb must come between the two lengths of the piece of cord.

As you bring your left hand away, use a French drop (see French Drop Vanish), so the ring falls into the palm of your right hand.

Pull on the sting and allow your thumb to come free. Tug the string a few times to mimic pulling the ring through the string.

Bring your left hand above your right and pretend to throw the ring back down onto the loop. As you do the throwing action, bring your right hand up and down quickly for cover.

On the down motion, push the ring down with your thumb so it drops to the bottom of the string loop.

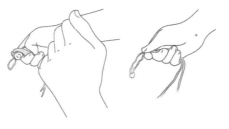

Related Chapters:

- French Drop Vanish

PENS

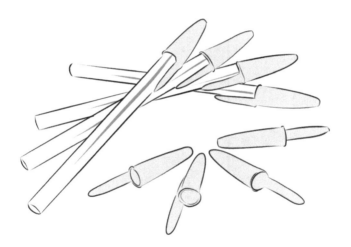

PEN-IN-PAPER VANISH

In this trick, you roll a pen up in a piece of paper, then scrunch up the paper to show the pen has disappeared.

Method

You need a pen and a piece of paper. Do this trick while sitting at an opaque table. Keep your knees together.

Roll the pen up inside the paper. Do so loosely, so the pen can move freely inside the paper. Twist one end of the paper closed.

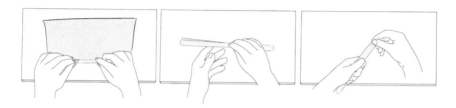

As you are doing so, allow the pen to fall out the other end into your lap.

With the pen out of the paper, twist the other end closed, then hold the paper between your two hands. On the count of three, crush the paper to show the pen has disappeared.

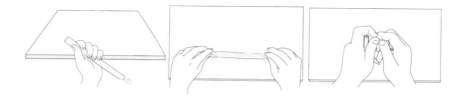

PEN-IN-LAP VANISH

In this trick, you hold a pen between your hands, and then it instantly vanishes as you clap your hands together.

Method

Do this trick while sitting at an opaque table. Keep your knees together.

Hold the pen horizontally between the palms of your hands. Keep it close to the edge of the table.

Bring your hands up and down three times. You can count aloud as you do it. On the third down movement, bring your hands together in a clapping motion.

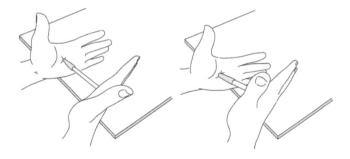

As you bring your hands together, move them backwards and release pressure on the pen so it falls into your lap.

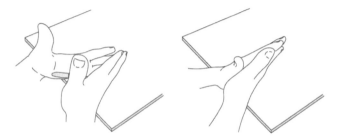

VANISHING PEN CAP

In this trick, you push a pen lid into your hand, but when you open your hand, the lid has disappeared.

Method

Hold the pen cap between your thumb, index, and middle fingers, and use your other hand to tap it down into your hand.

On the last tap, use your middle finger to push the cap forward so it pivots into a finger-palm in your tapping hand. A finger-palm is when you hold an object between the base and first knuckles of your fingers.

Show your hand empty.

To reproduce the cap, reach into the air as you let it fall into your fingers.

FLIP-STICK VANISH

With this trick, you make a pen vanish instantly, then reappear.

Method

Hold the pen horizontally by one end between your first finger, middle finger, and thumb. Bring your other hand over as if to grab the pen. This provides cover.

With your pen hand, extend your middle finger a little and use it to pull back on the pen. This is the flip-stick technique. Open your grabbing hand to show the pen has vanished.

To reproduce the pen, bring your hand back over to provide cover. Use your ring finger to push the pen to its original position as you slide your grabbing hand along it.

PEN TO COIN

Here, you make a pen instantly change into a coin.

Method

For this trick, you need a coin and a pen.

Hold a coin in the finger-palm position (see Vanishing Pen Cap) of one hand and a pen in your other hand, ready to do the flip-stick move (see Flip-Stick Vanish).

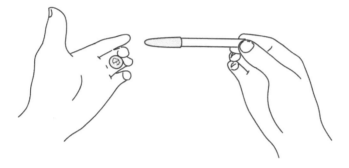

As you bring the hand holding the coin over to grab the pen, simultaneously make the pen vanish with the flip-stick technique and produce the coin from your finger-palm by sliding it with your thumb to your fingertips.

Reverse the actions to make it change back.

Related Chapters:

- Vanishing Pen Cap
- Flip-Stick Vanish

STRAWS

STRAW WAND

In this trick, you use a straw as a magic wand, and are able to make pieces of paper stick to it.

Method

This trick uses static electricity. You need a straw inside its paper wrapping. Open the straw and build up static electricity by rapidly moving it in and out of the paper several times.

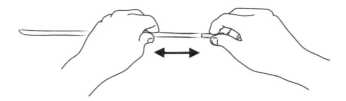

On the last pull, pull it off quickly.

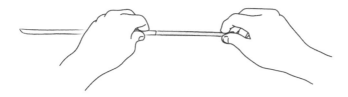

Now the straw has static charge. Get the straw paper and tear it up into little pieces. Bring the straw close to the pieces of paper, and they will stick to the straw.

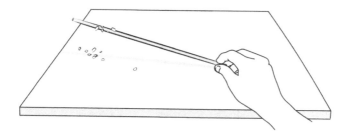

GHOST STRAW

In this trick, you place a straw on top of a bottle and are able to make it spin without touching it.

Method

This trick uses static electricity. You need a straw inside its paper cover and something to balance the straw on. A bottle works well.

Build up static electricity in the straw (see Straw Wand).

Balance the straw (without the paper) on the bottle. Slowly bring your hand towards the straw to make it rotate.

Related Chapters:

- Straw Wand

MAGNETIC STRAW

In this trick, you place a straw on a table and are able to move it without touching it.

Method

Place a straw on a flat surface and tell your spectator that you are going to use the power of magnetic fields to move it. Tell him to watch the straw carefully.

Use your hand to make a scraping motion on the table in front the straw. Motion away from, not toward, yourself. This motion is a redirection.

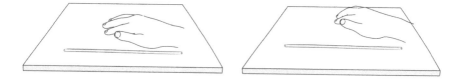

While the spectator is concentrating on the straw and your hand movement, blow lightly on the straw to make it move. Keep talking as you blow.

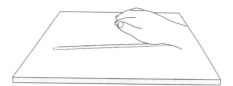

CROSSED STRAWS

In this trick, you twist two straws together and then are able to pull them apart through each other without breaking them.

Method

Get two straws and place one on top of the other to form a cross. The horizontal straw should be on top.

Do one full rotation with bottom straw around the top one.

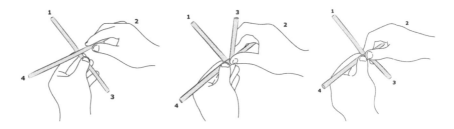

Twist the left side of the top straw around the center. As it reaches the bottom, twist the bottom part of the bottom straw up.

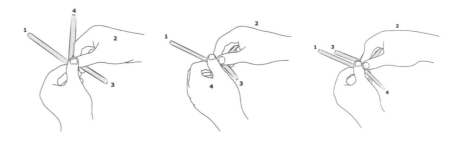

The motions look like you are creating a knot, but in reality, the second and third twists undo the first one.

Use your thumb and fingers in front of the "knot" to pinch it down.

Pretend to try pulling the straws apart a couple of times. The third time, let them separate. You will be left with two separate enclosed circles.

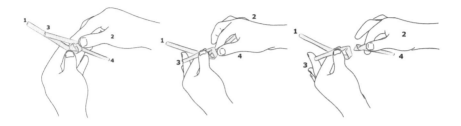

REPAIRING STRAW WRAPPER

In this trick, you tear a paper straw wrapper into little pieces. With a magical shake of your hands, it repairs itself.

Method

This trick uses two paper straw wrappings. While your spectator is not looking, roll one wrapping into a little ball and hide it in the fleshy part of your hand, between your thumb and index finger.

Tear up the other wrapping into little pieces in front of your spectator. Gather all the little pieces, crumple them into a little ball, and hold them up to show your spectator.

Bring your hands together and switch the torn pieces with the paper you hid in your hand. Disguise this switch by shaking your hands around as you do it. Unroll the un-torn wrapping and give it to the spectator to inspect.

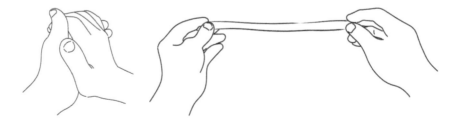

As he is inspecting the wrapper, get rid of the torn pieces by placing them in your pocket or dropping them to the ground.

ELASTIC BANDS

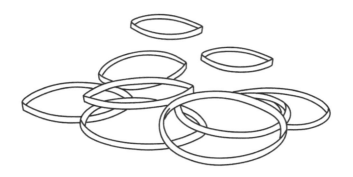

REPAIRING BAND

In this trick, you break an elastic band and then, with a magical shake of your hands, it repairs itself.

Method

Get an elastic band and put one end through the other end to create a doubled-up loop.

Hold the joint between your thumb and index finger of your left hand and stretch the band out so the two "strings" look like one. Do this by using all your fingers to pull it from the inside. Have both thumbs on top in the same position so it doesn't look suspicious.

Now pretend to snap the band in half. Pinch the band with you thumb and index finger of your right hand right next to your left thumb.

Pull the band until the two ends separate, giving the illusion of snapping it in half. Ensure the looped ends don't flash to the spectator.

Bring your two hands together with the "snapped" band between them. Shake your hands around, and then reveal it has repaired itself.

THUMB THROUGH BAND

In this illusion, you wrap an elastic band around your thumb and then pull it through your thumb without breaking it.

Method

The secret to this trick is in the way you wrap the elastic band around your thumb.

Put the band around the thumb, index, middle, and ring fingers of one hand. Place the thumb of your other hand between the ring finger and thumb of your first hand and stretch out the elastic band.

Turn your second hand over, and with your middle finger, grab the part of the band between your two thumbs.

Turn your hand back over so your middle finger is enclosed in the band. Take the thumb of your second hand and put it through the largest gap in the band (made by the fingers of your first hand).

Pull your middle finger out of its small loop. You will have a little knot. Keep tension on it so it doesn't come out.

Press your thumb against something to prove the band can't come off over it.

Release a little tension by bringing your hand closer to your thumb and the knot will unravel.

JUMPING BAND

In this trick, an elastic band is wrapped around two of your fingers and then "locked in" by a second elastic band twined over your fingertips. You open and close your fist and the first elastic band jumps from between your fingers.

Method

Get two elastic banks, preferably different of colors. Wrap one around your index and middle fingers twice. Wrap the second elastic band around your index finger and give it a twist.

Twist the second elastic band over each of your fingers in the same manner. Do not include your thumb.

Show your spectator the first elastic band is really on your fingers by pulling on it.

Turn your hand back around so your spectator can't see what you are doing. Close your fist so all four of your fingers go into the hole created by you pulling on the elastic band.

Quickly open your fist and close it again to make the elastic band "jump" over to your ring and pinky fingers. It will actually jump over just by opening your hand, but the quick open and close looks better.

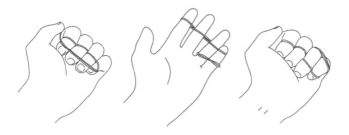

Here is what it looks like from the spectator's point of view.

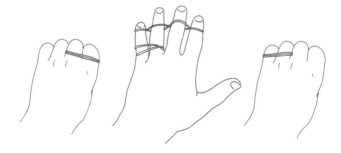

CROSSED BANDS

In this trick, two elastic bands are interlocked in your hands. After a quick rub, they magically separate without breaking or leaving your fingers.

Method

Get two elastic bands, preferably of different colors.

Wrap one elastic band around your thumb and index finger. Do the same with the one your other hand, but make it so the second band is interlocked with the first one. Stretch them apart to show that they are locked together.

Slide the second elastic band up and down the first one a few times to show that it is definitely "stuck."

As you reach the top of one of the slides, place one of your middle fingers on top of your index finger of the same hand.

Twist that hand over so your index finger slips out of the loop and your middle finger takes its place. Your index finger should go into the loop made by your thumb.

Take your middle finger out of the loop to separate the two elastic bands. Continue to rub them together a few times to add time between the release and the reveal.

Slowly separate the two elastic bands.

THANKS FOR READING

Dear reader,

Thank you for reading *Easy Magic Tricks*.

If you enjoyed this book, please leave a review where you bought it. It helps more than most people think.

Don't forget your FREE book chapters!

You will also be among the first to know of FREE review copies, discount offers, bonus content, and more.

Go to:

https://offers.SFNonfictionBooks.com/Free-Chapters

Thanks again for your support.

AUTHOR RECOMMENDATIONS

Teach Yourself Escape and Evasion Tactics

Discover the skills you need to evade and escape capture, because you never know when they will save your life.

Get it now.

www.SFNonfictionBooks.com/Evading-Escaping-Capture

ABOUT SAM FURY

Sam Fury has had a passion for survival, evasion, resistance, and escape (SERE) training since he was a young boy growing up in Australia.

This led him to years of training and career experience in related subjects, including martial arts, military training, survival skills, outdoor sports, and sustainable living.

These days, Sam spends his time refining existing skills, gaining new skills, and sharing what he learns via the Survival Fitness Plan website.

www.SurvivalFitnessPlan.com

Made in United States
Troutdale, OR
07/05/2023

10982429R00040